© **KEEP THE HOPE ALIVE**
BY SANDEEP RAVIDUTT SHARMA

Table of Contents

Introduction IV

Keep The Hope Alive.......................... 1

© KEEP THE HOPE ALIVE
BY SANDEEP RAVIDUTT SHARMA

Introduction

This book provides you with a list of **100 motivational quotes and thoughts** focussing mainly on improving your wellness quotient. Sometimes you don't see yourself clearly in the mirror, either you are still in the sleep mode, or you forgot to clean the mirror surface. Be ready in any situation and never lose hope. Life unfolds every minute throwing surprises and shocks. Keep the hope alive even when you have fallen in the deepest pit. Let the candle of positivity kindle the hope of prosperity. You need to prepare your mind to receive the riches of the world with grace and patience. The positive thoughts go a long way in keeping the hope alive. I'm sure if you keep reading, referring, sharing these thoughts and quotes, you may derive inspiration and develop a good understanding of various perspectives and facts of life.

"Let the candle of hope burn and illuminate your mind."

I sincerely hope, you will find this book amazing, interesting, rejuvenating, unique and constant source of inspiration.

Thank You and Happy Reading.

KEEP THE HOPE ALIVE

© **KEEP THE HOPE ALIVE**
BY SANDEEP RAVIDUTT SHARMA

Have faith in the Lord, and your prayers will be answered soon.

© **KEEP THE HOPE ALIVE**
BY SANDEEP RAVIDUTT SHARMA

Those who sway their torch while walking in the dark to show the way for others are kind.

© **KEEP THE HOPE ALIVE**
BY SANDEEP RAVIDUTT SHARMA

Get ready to receive the power of knowledge and happiness through the bridge of kindness and blessings.

© **KEEP THE HOPE ALIVE**
BY SANDEEP RAVIDUTT SHARMA

When you combine youth with experience. Success is likely.

© KEEP THE HOPE ALIVE
BY SANDEEP RAVIDUTT SHARMA

Your first win in the gamble gets permanently registered in your mind and doesn't get erased with hundreds of losses. You start believing in recovering all your losses in the next attempt. Don't get glued to gambling of any kind. Achieve through your efforts.

© **KEEP THE HOPE ALIVE**
BY SANDEEP RAVIDUTT SHARMA

An attitude to take revenge doesn't help. It ultimately puts you to sail in drowning Titanic. Forgive and grow lighter.

You need to learn or use smart ways to convey the seriousness of any kind in the lighter vein.

Time becomes precious or wasteful based on how you use it to make your life better and beautiful.

© **KEEP THE HOPE ALIVE**
BY SANDEEP RAVIDUTT SHARMA

As the day begins, life takes a new turn and gets ready for the shocks and surprises. Each day brings with it lots of choices for you to make. You gain or lose based on the choices you make every day. Wish you a great day full of happiness and order in life.

Appreciate good deeds of others in time. This could motivate the doer towards excellence.

© **KEEP THE HOPE ALIVE**
BY SANDEEP RAVIDUTT SHARMA

Shadows do not last for long. If noone is there to walk with you, the shadow keeps trailing you or moving forward. You are never left alone by the Lord who holds your hand every minute. Thanks for the concern...O dear God...

© **KEEP THE HOPE ALIVE**
BY SANDEEP RAVIDUTT SHARMA

With just one win you can erase your hundred failures.

There is no place on this earth and the entire universe, where the will and grace of God don't exist. All you need is pure thoughts and complete surrender to the almighty to experience the same.

Never wait for the perfect plan instead execute the plan perfectly.

© **KEEP THE HOPE ALIVE**
BY SANDEEP RAVIDUTT SHARMA

Showers of light illuminate our world.

Your success has already proved your credentials. Now the challenge is to maintain or grow from this point.

© **KEEP THE HOPE ALIVE**
BY SANDEEP RAVIDUTT SHARMA

Beautiful pathways are always built on difficult terrain. Overcoming difficulties in life initially lead to smooth pathways later.

Give respect and take respect is not just a slogan but should be the way of life.

© **KEEP THE HOPE ALIVE**
BY SANDEEP RAVIDUTT SHARMA

Let's remember we are here to live happily. So bury all your differences and learn to live and let live.

Hatred only likes itself whereas Love even likes Hatred.

Salvation keeps knocking on your door but it seems you are yet to focus like Buddha.

The path of truth places obstacles to test your resolve.

© **KEEP THE HOPE ALIVE**
BY SANDEEP RAVIDUTT SHARMA

Rope can connect people, things or places. It can also hang someone. Use it wisely.

Give up your sadness, ego and expectations. Be happy.

Get the magic of positive thinking, and you no more need a miracle.

© KEEP THE HOPE ALIVE
BY SANDEEP RAVIDUTT SHARMA

You are yet to reach your destination. Get up now, its a new day, cover up distance for the day with full energy and enthusiasm. Today is your day.

© **KEEP THE HOPE ALIVE**
BY SANDEEP RAVIDUTT SHARMA

Bury your past if it stinks. Get ready to embrace the colourful future by focusing on today.

© KEEP THE HOPE ALIVE
BY SANDEEP RAVIDUTT SHARMA

© Copyright 2018 Sandeep Ravidutt Sharma - All rights reserved.

In no way is it legal to reproduce, duplicate, or transmit any part of this document in either electronic means or in printed format. Recording of this publication is strictly prohibited and any storage of this document is not allowed unless with written permission from the publisher. All rights reserved. The information provided herein is stated to be truthful and consistent, in that any liability, in terms of inattention or otherwise, by any usage or abuse of any policies, processes, or directions contained within is the solitary and utter responsibility of the recipient reader. Under no circumstances will any legal responsibility or blame be held against the author / publisher for any reparation, damages, or monetary loss due to the information herein, either directly or indirectly. The author own all copyrights.

Legal Notice:
This book is copyright protected. This is only for personal use. You cannot amend, distribute, sell, use, quote or paraphrase any part or the content within this book without the consent of the author or copyright owner. Legal action will be pursued if this is breached.

Disclaimer Notice:
Please note the information contained within this book is for motivational, educational and knowledge sharing purpose only. Every attempt has been made to provide the reader accurate, up to date and reliable complete information. No warranties of any kind are expressed or implied. Readers acknowledge that the author is not engaging in the rendering of legal, financial, medical or professional advice. By reading this document, the reader agrees that under no circumstances the author / publisher is responsible for any losses, direct or indirect, which are incurred as a result of the use of information contained within this document, including, but not limited to, —errors, omissions, or inaccuracies.

If you have further questions, contact on
Tel: +919969256731
Email: sandeepraviduttsharma@gmail.com

© KEEP THE HOPE ALIVE
BY SANDEEP RAVIDUTT SHARMA

Dedication

This book is dedicated to **Goddess Bhairavi**. In the Hindu religion, the Goddess Bhairavi represents divine anger and wrath which is directed towards impurities within us as well as to the negative forces that obstructs our spiritual growth. Bhairavi Mata is also called as **Shubhamkari** and does good things. She is often depicted in images as holding a book, rosary and making abhaya and varada mudra with her hands. She is fiercely protective, lending us wisdom and power, steadiness and clarity. She personifies light and fire, supporting us to reveal what we keep hidden and inviting us to explore our hidden mind and any secret darkness.

I hereby recite the following Bhairavi mool mantra...
"Om Hreem Bhairavi Kalaum Hreem Svaha"
And pray to **Goddess Bhairavi** for lending wisdom and power, steadiness and clarity in the life of my readers and the world. May Goddess Bhairavi protect us from negative forces along with removing impurities of our mind.

© **KEEP THE HOPE ALIVE**
BY SANDEEP RAVIDUTT SHARMA

You may look similar to others. But remember you and your life path are always different and unique.

Don't assume but earn happiness.

© **KEEP THE HOPE ALIVE**
BY SANDEEP RAVIDUTT SHARMA

The invisible hand of the Lord always protects you from failing and falling. Be thankful to the Lord.

© KEEP THE HOPE ALIVE
BY SANDEEP RAVIDUTT SHARMA

Share your joy with others, and it would multiply manifolds.

Each one of us is a unique creation of the almighty God. Don't attempt to compare one with the other. A comparison would invite unhappiness for all concerned.

The power of prayer cannot be fully explained but can be experienced.

You are the one who has the power to create Good Times.

Revise your expectations if you have facts and figures about your current achievements.

© **KEEP THE HOPE ALIVE**
BY SANDEEP RAVIDUTT SHARMA

Moments of yesterday become stories of today.

© KEEP THE HOPE ALIVE
BY SANDEEP RAVIDUTT SHARMA

Rose and thorns are inseparable. Our life mimics nature. Happiness and grief are part of our lives.

© KEEP THE HOPE ALIVE
BY SANDEEP RAVIDUTT SHARMA

Truth has many faces for each one of us. Based on your knowledge and understanding, you may consider certain things as truth but for the other truth may have some other face. No one in this world has seen a complete truth, still, we believe our version of Truth to be the truth.

Time makes you laugh and cry.

© **KEEP THE HOPE ALIVE**
BY SANDEEP RAVIDUTT SHARMA

Hug yourself in the mirror and smile before you start your day.

© KEEP THE HOPE ALIVE
BY SANDEEP RAVIDUTT SHARMA

Time is always right for you when you are not ashamed of any misdeeds. You are proud and confident about your existence. Pride comes from your kindness and good deeds. You need to start living your life not only to make you happy but to wipe out tears from the faces of those who are left out stranded.

© **KEEP THE HOPE ALIVE**
BY SANDEEP RAVIDUTT SHARMA

Believe in your self. Don't bother too much about what others have to say about you.

© **KEEP THE HOPE ALIVE**
BY SANDEEP RAVIDUTT SHARMA

Get out of the chaos of the past and noises of the future. Live NOW.

© **KEEP THE HOPE ALIVE**
BY SANDEEP RAVIDUTT SHARMA

Success likes your name.

Anticipate good things in life but not without putting in efforts to achieve it.

© **KEEP THE HOPE ALIVE**
BY SANDEEP RAVIDUTT SHARMA

If you close your eyes that doesn't mean that the world ceases to exist, the sun will not rise again and Sky would freeze. We all are interlinked with the forces of this universe, but our existence is independent of each other.

Pathways can be big or small, but it always takes you to some destination.

Time heals everything.

KEEP THE HOPE ALIVE
BY SANDEEP RAVIDUTT SHARMA

You don't have to worry about what will happen tomorrow, provided you focus on your efforts today.

You no longer remain wrong if you have accepted your fault.

Cheer up if you are sad. It's not the end of the world.

© **KEEP THE HOPE ALIVE**
BY SANDEEP RAVIDUTT SHARMA

Be selfish when you want peace of mind.

Trust someone who is an achiever, and who frankly shares his learning from failures.

Get ready to face the world and make your life beautiful.

Anyway, the dust will settle down after the storm. Have patience.

KEEP THE HOPE ALIVE
BY SANDEEP RAVIDUTT SHARMA

Stars twinkle for you to smile or as you smile, stars twinkle. Whatever may be the case. Keep smiling.

© **KEEP THE HOPE ALIVE**
BY SANDEEP RAVIDUTT SHARMA

You need to speak aloud when someone is trying to suppress your freedom.

Not everyone can become Buddha but if you have decided, no one can stop you to attain enlightenment.

© **KEEP THE HOPE ALIVE**
BY SANDEEP RAVIDUTT SHARMA

Those who attempt to rewrite or distort history in their own way should understand that they cannot undo the contribution of people of the past. It's better to focus on what you can do today rather than work to discredit the ones who are now part of the history.

Give work instead of alms to poor brethren.

Reveal your positive side not just for a day but throughout your lifetime.

Erase self-doubt and write self-belief in your mind.

© **KEEP THE HOPE ALIVE**
BY SANDEEP RAVIDUTT SHARMA

Those who spend their time finding faults in others get the garbage in return. Appreciate the contribution of others and attract positivity in place of looking for faults.

© KEEP THE HOPE ALIVE
BY SANDEEP RAVIDUTT SHARMA

At times you are all alone to push forward your life. Keep Going.

Friends are forever for the fortunate ones.

© **KEEP THE HOPE ALIVE**
BY SANDEEP RAVIDUTT SHARMA

When words can't console, practice silence.

© **KEEP THE HOPE ALIVE**
BY SANDEEP RAVIDUTT SHARMA

Throw all the garbage out of your mind in case you have accumulated due to unpleasant past experience. Embrace positivity and make your life beautiful.

© **KEEP THE HOPE ALIVE**
BY SANDEEP RAVIDUTT SHARMA

Our thoughts make us what we are.

© **KEEP THE HOPE ALIVE**
BY SANDEEP RAVIDUTT SHARMA

Your life path and journey are never just black and white. Each step forward reveals a new colour.

You can't simply stand at the crossroads permanently. Sooner or later you will have to choose your path and continue your life journey.

© **KEEP THE HOPE ALIVE**
BY SANDEEP RAVIDUTT SHARMA

Throwing a stone in the river can only create ripples and not the waves of the Ocean. Your volume of efforts decides the impact.

© **KEEP THE HOPE ALIVE**
BY SANDEEP RAVIDUTT SHARMA

Greet everyone you meet with a smile and discuss how you can make lives of one and all better.

© **KEEP THE HOPE ALIVE**
BY SANDEEP RAVIDUTT SHARMA

Running faster makes you the winner but not the winner forever. Win the hearts with your kindness, and your win is forever.

Give respect to others and earn respect in return.

Believe in your own words rather than try to decipher speeches of others.

Destruction is the end of a phase and marks the beginning of a new one. Sometimes destruction is the only way for new creation.

Be happy with what you have, rather than mourn on what you expected and could not get.

You earn or learn based on your understanding and attitude.

© **KEEP THE HOPE ALIVE**
BY SANDEEP RAVIDUTT SHARMA

For most of us talks remain friendly till the time the other person is listening. Let each speak in turn, and the other listens if you really want to be friends.

Don't assume things in life.

Blessed are those souls who are able to catch the divine signal.

Your intentions in any project influence the outcome.

Be kind when you can see a lot of tears spilling eyes all around.

© **KEEP THE HOPE ALIVE**
BY SANDEEP RAVIDUTT SHARMA

Take a trip to the island of your thoughts and come back with the positive ones.

Thoughts become meaningful when supported by action in time.

© KEEP THE HOPE ALIVE
BY SANDEEP RAVIDUTT SHARMA

The sky looks into the mirror. Cloud changes it's make up every minute, birds crisscross in between to get a glimpse. So what are you waiting for, take a dip into the sea and grab them all.

If you find hurdles in your path to success. Focus on what you want to achieve and get ready to roll over the hurdles like a road roller.

Forgiveness sets you free. Forgiveness makes you lighter at heart and richer in mind.

© **KEEP THE HOPE ALIVE**
BY SANDEEP RAVIDUTT SHARMA

You can hit the target if everything else blurs out in front of you. Focus on your target.

© **KEEP THE HOPE ALIVE**
BY SANDEEP RAVIDUTT SHARMA

Time is the greatest teacher. It teaches you every minute and constantly takes your test so that you score high in your life test.

© **KEEP THE HOPE ALIVE**
BY SANDEEP RAVIDUTT SHARMA

Expressing your gratitude or giving thanks creates a positive energy field around you.

© KEEP THE HOPE ALIVE
BY SANDEEP RAVIDUTT SHARMA

Stones have the patience to lie at one place for hundreds of years and display extreme calmness. But if the same stone is put into motion on a hilltop, it rolls down in anger and can damage anything coming its way.

© **KEEP THE HOPE ALIVE**
BY SANDEEP RAVIDUTT SHARMA

Be a bee which collects honey every minute from the flowers so that your child can sleep well or you live long.

© KEEP THE HOPE ALIVE
BY SANDEEP RAVIDUTT SHARMA

Most of us likes to give or receive beautiful flowers grown by others. Only those who love, nurture and grow them, really knows the pain of plucking and parting with them.

© KEEP THE HOPE ALIVE
BY SANDEEP RAVIDUTT SHARMA

You can do no wrong if you are conscious of this fact.

Choose the right wish and it will be fulfilled. Kind is always right.

© **KEEP THE HOPE ALIVE**
BY SANDEEP RAVIDUTT SHARMA

Time beams you among the less fortunate ones to hear their story and become their saviour.

© **KEEP THE HOPE ALIVE**
BY SANDEEP RAVIDUTT SHARMA

Let the arrogant sleep while humanity lives joyfully.

When you donate for some good cause, not only the recipient benefits but you also benefit a lot in terms of blessings, attract positive vibes, and improve your happiness quotient.

World cheers for winners who did their best in worst times.

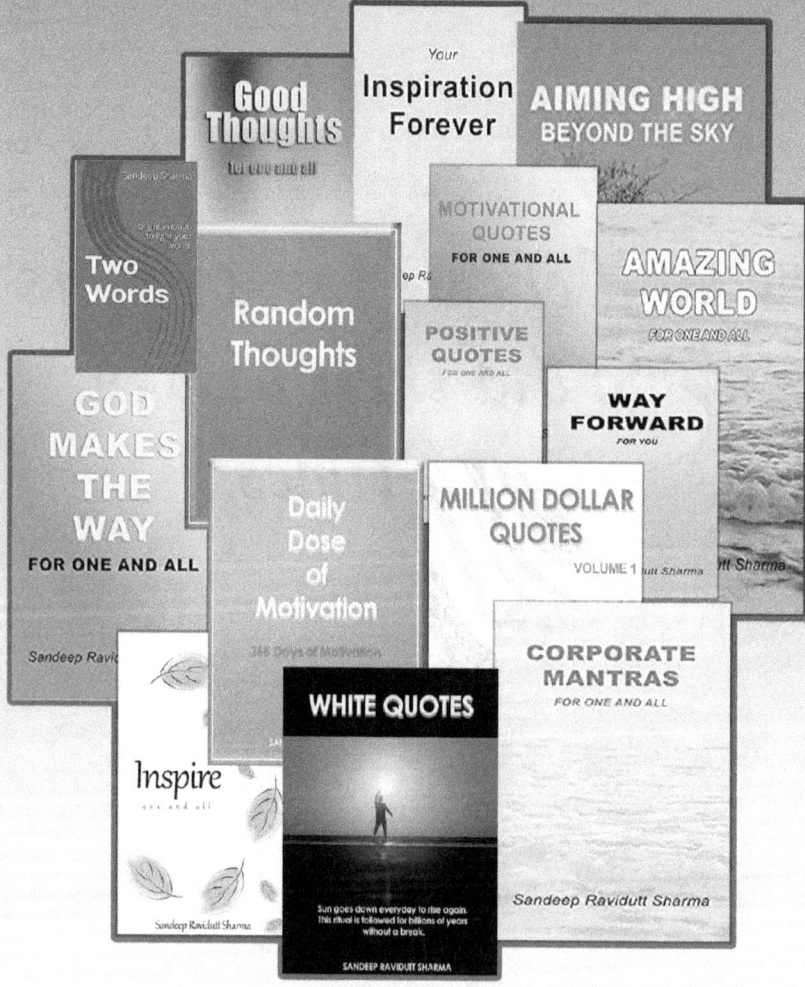

www.ingramcontent.com/pod-product-compliance
Lightning Source LLC
Chambersburg PA
CBHW070803220526
45466CB00002B/526